FRANCHISING IN TUNISIA 2014

Legal and Business Considerations

KENDAL H. TYRE, JR., EXECUTIVE EDITOR
DIANA VILMENAY-HAMMOND, MANAGING EDITOR
COURTNEY L. LINDSAY II, ASSISTANT EDITOR

LEXNOIR FOUNDATION

FIRST QUARTER 2014

LexNoir Foundation is the charitable, educational arm of LexNoir, an international network of lawyers connecting the African Diaspora.

This publication, *Franchising in Tunisia 2014: Legal and Business Considerations*, contains excerpts from *Franchising in Africa 2014: Legal and Business Considerations*. Both works are published by LexNoir Foundation and reflect the points of view of the authors and editors as of the date of publication and do not necessarily represent the opinions, interpretations, or positions of the law firms or organizations with which they are affiliated, nor the opinions, interpretations or positions of LexNoir Foundation or LexNoir.

Nothing contained in this book is to be considered as the rendering of legal advice, either generally or in connection with any specific issues or case. Readers are responsible for obtaining advice from their own legal counsel or other professional. This book, any forms and agreements or other information herein are intended for educational and informational purposes only.

www.lexnoir.org

Table of Contents

About the Editors and Authors iv

About the Book.. viii

Franchising in Tunisia

Yessine Ferah
FERAH & Associates Law Firm

I.   Introduction 1

      A.   Historical Background of Country 1
      B.   Economy of Country 1
      C.   Franchise Legal Overview 2

II.   Regulatory Requirements 3

      A.   Pre-Sale Disclosure 3
      B.   Governmental Approvals, Registrations, Filing
           Requirements 4
           1.   Authorization of the Trade Minister 5
           2.   The Central Bank of Tunisia's Prior Authorization 9
           3.   Registration before the Tax Office 11
      C.   Limits of Fees and Typical Term of Franchise
           Agreement 11

III. Currency 11

IV.   Taxes, Tariffs and Duties... 11

V.   Trademarks 12

VI.   Restrictions on Transfer.. 13

VII. Termination 14

      A.   Termination from the Competition Law Perspective 14
      B.   Termination under the Insolvency Legal Regime 15
      C.   Termination from a Civil Law Perspective 15

VIII. Governing Law, Jurisdiction, and Dispute Resolution 16

      A.   Choice of Law of Foreign Jurisdiction................. 16
      B.   International Arbitration Dispute Resolution 17

IX.   Non-Competition Provisions 18

X.   Language Requirements 18

XI. Other Significant Matters.. 19

Bibliography of International Franchise Resources

Kendal H. Tyre, Jr., Diana Vilmenay-Hammond, Pierce Haesung
Han, Courtney L. Lindsay II and Keri McWilliams
Nixon Peabody LLP

I. General International Resources 23

II. African Resources... 26

    A. Angola... 27

    B. Botswana... 28

    C. Cape Verde.. 28

    D. Egypt 28

    E. Ethiopia 28

    F. Ghana 28

    G. Libya 29

    H. Mozambique.. 29

    I. Nigeria.. 29

    J. South Africa 29

    K. Tunisia.. 30

    L. Zambia 30

Acknowledgment

This book could not have been written without the hard work and dedication of each of the contributing authors and editors. Thank you.

We would like to acknowledge and extend our heartfelt gratitude to Michael Collier and Maria Stallings of the Washington, D.C. office of Nixon Peabody LLP for their invaluable assistance in revising, proofing, and editing this publication.

About the Editors and Authors

Kendal H. Tyre, Jr. – Kendal is a partner in the Washington, D.C. office of Nixon Peabody LLP. He handles domestic and cross-border transactions, including mergers and acquisitions, joint ventures, strategic alliances, licensing, and franchise matters.

In his franchise and licensing practice, Kendal counsels domestic and international franchisors, franchisees, licensors, licensees and distributors regarding U.S. state and federal franchise laws as well as foreign franchise legislation in a variety of jurisdictions. Kendal drafts and provides advice with regard to franchise and license agreements, disclosure documents and area development agreements and has extensive experience drafting and negotiating a variety of other commercial agreements. His client base spans the United States and foreign countries, including South Africa, Kenya, and the United Kingdom.

Kendal is a frequent contributor to franchise publications and a frequent speaker at franchise programs held by the American Bar Association Forum on Franchising and the International Franchise Association.

Kendal is co-chair of the firm's Diversity Action Committee and its Africa Group. Kendal is also the executive director of LexNoir Foundation.

E-mail address: ktyre@nixonpeabody.com

Diana Vilmenay-Hammond – Diana is an attorney in the Washington, D.C. office of Nixon Peabody LLP. She is a member of the firm's Franchise & Distribution Team.

In her franchise practice, Diana works with domestic and international franchisors on transactional and litigation matters. Specifically, she counsels franchisor clients regarding state and federal franchise laws, disclosure and registration obligations.

Diana drafts and negotiates various commercial agreements, including international franchise and development agreements.

Diana has co-authored numerous articles on franchising and frequently co-hosted the Nixon Peabody franchise law webinar series. Topics have included:

- "Franchise Case Law Round-Up: Implications for Your Franchise," February 15, 2012;
- "Social Media Part II: Best Practices in Protecting Your Brand in the New Media," September 14, 2010; and
- "The Awuah Case: Bellwether or Outlier," May 11, 2010

Diana received her J.D. from Howard University School of Law and her B.A. from Georgetown University. She is a member of the American Bar Association (Forum on Franchising).

Email address: dvilmenay@nixonpeabody.com

Pierce Haesung Han – Pierce is an associate in Nixon Peabody's Global Business & Transactions Group. Pierce focuses his practice on three main areas, assisting clients with a variety of complex business transactions.

- Mergers & Acquisitions: Providing assistance to both public and private clients with various mergers and acquisitions, performing due diligence, drafting and negotiating transaction documents, and facilitating closing and post-closing mechanics.
- International Commercial Transactions: Drafting and negotiating a variety of commercial agreements, including international franchise and development agreements, license agreements, and purchase and sale agreements.
- Federal Securities Law Matters: Assisting public and private clients regarding federal securities laws and stock exchange rules relating to corporate governance and disclosure.

Pierce serves as the Secretary of the Asian Pacific Bar Association Educational Fund (an affiliate of the Asian Pacific American Bar Association of the Greater Washington, D.C. Area).

Pierce received his J.D. from Georgetown University Law Center and his B.A. from Case Western Reserve University. He is admitted to practice in the State of New York and the District of Columbia.

E-mail address: phan@nixonpeabody.com

Courtney L. Lindsay, II – Courtney is an associate in Nixon Peabody's Corporate and Finance practice. In his corporate practice, Courtney assists for-profit and non-profit entities with transactional matters and corporate governance. In various capacities, Courtney has been involved in multiple merger and acquisition transactions, including drafting and managing due diligence.

Previously, Courtney worked in the legal and business affairs department at a national cable network, where he handled matters related to the network's LLC agreement, including drafting board and member consent agreements.

Courtney received his J.D. from the University of Virginia School of Law and his B.A. from the University of Virginia. He is admitted to practice in the Commonwealth of Virginia and the District of Columbia.

E-mail address: clindsay@nixonpeabody.com

Keri McWilliams – Keri is an associate in the Franchise & Distribution team of Nixon Peabody LLP. Keri works with clients on a number of franchising issues, including obtaining and maintaining franchise registrations in various states, responding to state inquiries regarding trade practices, ongoing compliance with state and federal regulations, and updating franchise disclosure documents. She also handles franchise sales counseling and franchise system issues.

Keri is a member of the American Bar Association's Forum on Franchising, and the Federal and Minnesota State bar associations. She is also a member of Minnesota Women Lawyers and the Minnesota Association of Black Lawyers, and a volunteer in the Volunteer Lawyers Network.

Keri received her J.D. from the Georgetown University Law Center and her B.F.A. from Washington University. She is admitted to practice in the District of Columbia and Minnesota.

E-mail address: kmcwilliams@nixonpeabody.com

Yessine Ferah – Yessine is the Managing Director of FERAH & Associates Law Firm in Tunis, Tunisia. He is a tax and corporate lawyer with specialization in large-scale commercial transactions. He has many years of experience representing major multinational companies in private and public domestic and cross-border mergers and acquisitions, joint ventures and alliances, tax strategy, banking and finance, and complex commercial agreements. He has been counsel on a number of transactions within energy (oil, gas, and electricity), telecommunications, banking, and tourism industries.

Yessine obtained the post-graduate qualification (DEA) in law from the University of Legal, Political, and Social Sciences of Tunis-University of Tunis, and is currently working toward a Ph.D. in law at the University of Paris I Panthéon-Sorbonne. He also attended the 2004 Program of Instruction for Lawyers at Harvard Law School. He is a member of the Association of International Petroleum Negotiators, the Chambre Tuniso-Française de Commerce et d'Industrie, and the Bar Association of Tunisia.

E-mail address: yessine.ferah@fandalawfirm.com

About the Book

Franchising in Tunisia 2014: Legal and Business Considerations contains excerpts from the larger work, *Franchising in Africa 2014: Legal and Business Considerations*. Both books serve as practical, succinct, easy-to-use reference tools for lawyers, business people and academics to use in navigating the myriad laws and business issues impacting franchise arrangements on the African continent.

This book provides an overview of the franchise industry in Tunisia and addresses the typical legal issues confronted when expanding a franchise system in Tunisia. The larger work, *Franchising in Africa 2014: Legal and Business Considerations*, covers those laws governing franchising in fifteen other African countries – Angola, Botswana, Burundi, Cape Verde, Democratic Republic of Congo, Egypt, Ethiopia, Ghana, Kenya, Mozambique, Nigeria, Rwanda, South Africa, Zambia and Zimbabwe.

In both books, an author, who is a legal expert in the designated jurisdiction, addresses the basic questions that a franchise lawyer would need to know to competently represent a client in expanding their franchise system to that country.

Each country chapter organizes a discussion of that country's laws under various headings and in a uniform format. Topics were sent to each country's author in the form of a questionnaire, and each author drafted responses to the questions presented. A general overview relating to the political and economic history of the country at the beginning of each chapter provides an initial context for the regulatory framework. [1]

---

[1] The source of information for these sections is the Central Intelligence Agency, https://www.cia.gov/library/publications/the-world-factbook/ (last visited November 3, 2013).

Apart from an overview of the legal framework for franchising, each book contains other articles and resources that should prove useful to those in the franchise industry.

The authors for each chapter are listed at the beginning of a chapter and their biographical information is listed in the previous section, *About the Editors and Authors*.

Readers should always consult with local counsel in the relevant jurisdiction instead of relying solely on the information contained in this book. The laws governing franchising are evolving and local counsel in Tunisia are best positioned to provide timely, relevant advice applying the current law to the particular facts of a case.

Franchising in Tunisia

Yessine Ferah

FERAH & Associates Law Firm

Tunis, Tunisia

Tunisia

I. Introduction

A. Historical Background of Country

Tunisia became an independent state in 1956. The country's first president, Habib Bourguiba, established a strict one-party state. He dominated the country for 31 years, repressing Islamic fundamentalism and establishing rights for women. In November 1987, Bourguiba was removed from office and replaced by Zine el Abidine Ben Ali in a coup. Street protests that began in Tunis in December 2010 over high unemployment, corruption, widespread poverty, and high food prices escalated in January 2011, culminating in rioting that led to hundreds of deaths. On January 14, 2011, the same day Ben Ali dismissed the government, he fled the country, and by late January 2011, Prime Minister Mohamed Ghannouchi announced the formation of a "national unity government" with the head of the Chamber of Deputies, Fouad M'Bazaa, as the interim president. Elections for the new Constituent Assembly were held in late October 2011, and in December, it elected human rights activist Moncef Marzouki as interim president. The Consistent Assembly adopted a new constitution on January 26, 2014. The Independent High Committee for the Elections anticipated that the presidential and parliamentary elections would be held before the end of 2014.

B. Economy of Country

Tunisia has a diverse, market-oriented economy, with important agricultural, mining, tourism, and manufacturing sectors but it faces an array of challenges. Following an ill-fated experiment with socialist economic policies in the 1960s, Tunisia successfully focused on bolstering exports, foreign investment, and tourism. Key exports now include textiles and apparel, food products, petroleum products, chemicals, and phosphates, with about 80% going to the European Union. Tunisia achieved four decades of 4-5% annual GDP growth. The overthrow of the government in January 2011 sent Tunisia's economy into a tailspin. The country's new government faces immediate

1

Tunisia

challenges stabilizing the economy. It must reassure businesses and investors, bring budget and current account deficits under control, shore up the country's financial system, bring down high unemployment, and reduce economic disparities between the more developed coastal region and the impoverished interior.

C.   Franchise Legal Overview

Before August 12, 2009, a franchise agreement in Tunisia was considered a sui generis contract governed primarily by the general legal regime applicable to contracted obligations under the *Tunisian Civil Code* (*Code des Obligations et des Contrats*).

Currently, *Law n° 2009-69*, dated August 12, 2009 (the "2009 Law"), regulates franchise agreements. The 2009 Law defines franchise agreements and stipulates the principal requirements to be fulfilled in a franchise relationship.

Article 14 of the 2009 Law defines the franchise agreement as "a contract through which the trademark owner grants the right of its use to a natural person or to a legal entity called franchisee, to distribute the products or provide services in return for consideration." Article 14 also provides that a "franchise network" consists of independent shops operating under the same trademark and pursuant to unified business methods, premises planning, management methods, marketing and sources of supply.

Article 15 of the 2009 Law and *Decree n° 2010-1501* (the "Decree"), which was enacted on June 21, 2010, provides compulsory terms and conditions of a franchise agreement. It also lists the basic information that must be included in a pre-sale disclosure document that must be provided to the franchisee at least twenty (20) days before signing the franchise agreement.

Article 6 of Tunisia's competition law ("Competition Law") provides that a franchise agreement is not deemed anticompetitive, if the parties justify that the franchise agreement is necessary to guarantee technical or economic progress and if

2

Tunisia

the agreement provides users with a fair share of benefits. Such franchise agreements, however, remain subject to the authorization of the Trade Minister of Tunisia, pursuant to the advice of the Competition Council of Tunisia.[2] On July 28, 2010, the Trade Minister of Tunisia enacted an order (the "Trade Minister Order") relating to the automatic authorization of some franchise agreements in specific industry sectors.

II.   Regulatory Requirements

A.   Pre-Sale Disclosure

Please describe any pre-sale franchise disclosure or similar requirements that may apply to franchise transactions.

Article 15 of the 2009 Law and the Decree require that the franchisor provide to the franchisee the franchise agreement and a disclosure document containing certain information relating to the franchisor and its activity at least twenty (20) days before signing the franchise agreement.

Article 3 of the Decree provides that the disclosure document must include:

- the legal form of the franchisor's enterprise and the nature of its activity;

- the identity and address of the franchisor, if the franchisor is a natural person;

- the identity of the legal representative, the head office address, the list of managers/directors and franchisor's amount of capital, if the franchisor is a legal entity;

---

[2]   The Competition Law was adopted by the *Law n° 91-64* dated 29 July 1991. It has been amended in 1993, 1995, 1999, 2003 and 2005.

- a presentation of the history of the franchisor's enterprise;

- information related to the franchisor's registration number in the trade register (or any equivalent registration number);

- proof of ownership of the trademark or the corporate name;

- information relating to the registration of the trademark with the national register of trademarks;

- information about the franchise network;

- the list of franchisees in Tunisia, their addresses, dates on which they joined the franchise network and a list of former franchisees;

- information about the franchisor's activity sector and the opportunities in Tunisia and other areas where the mark is represented;

- the nature and the amount of expenses and investment specific to the trademark or the corporate name; and

- the financial statements of the franchisor.

B.   Governmental Approvals, Registrations, Filing Requirements

Please describe any necessary government approvals, registrations, or filing requirements that may apply to franchise transactions.

Tunisia

1.   Authorization of the Trade Minister

Certain franchise agreements, depending on the industry in which they operate, may require the authorization of the Trade Minister of Tunisia prior to their execution. The relevant legislation in this area is Article 5 and Article 6 of the Competition Law, the Decree and the Trade Minister Order.

a.   Article 5 of the Competition Law

Article 5 of the Competition Law prohibits joint operations, collusion and express or tacit agreements that have an anti-competitive objective or effect and which:

- obstruct price setting by the rule of supply and demand;

- limit access to the market by other enterprises or limit the free exercise of competition in that market;

- either limit or control production, commercialization, investments, or technical progress; or

- divide markets or sources of supply.

Article 5 of the Competition Law also prohibits:

- abuse of a dominant position in the domestic market or a substantial part of that market, or abuse of a state of economic dependency of customers or suppliers who do not have any alternative solutions for commercialization, supply or provision of service. Abuse of a state of economic dependency may consist notably of the refusal to sell or to purchase tied goods or services, the imposition of de minimus prices for resale, discriminatory conditions, or the termination of commercial relationships without objective cause or because the other party refused to accept exorbitant commercial conditions;

- any offer or application of prices so abusively low that they threaten the balance of economic activity and honest competition on the market; and

- any engagement, convention or contractual clause relating to the practices prohibited under the terms of this Section.

b. Article 6 of the Competition Law

Article 6 of the Competition Law provides that certain agreements and practices are not considered anticompetitive if they guarantee technical or economic progress and provide users with a fair share of benefits. Such agreements and practices are subject to the authorization of the Trade Minister, after consultation with the Competition Council of Tunisia.

c. Application of Articles 5 and 6 of the Competition Law

It follows from a combined reading of the provisions of the Decree and Articles 5 and 6 of the Competition Law that all franchise agreement are in principle prohibited by Article 5 of the Competition Law; however, franchise agreements may be authorized by the Trade Minister, if they fulfill the conditions of Article 6 of the Competition Law.

d. Trade Minister Order

Notwithstanding Articles 5 and 6 of the Competition Law, franchise agreements in certain activity sectors determined by order of the Trade Minister will be automatically authorized and

Tunisia

do not require any further approval of the Trade Minister.[3] These sectors are set by the Trade Minister Order and are referenced below. For national brands, all sectors are automatically authorized. For foreign brands, only the following sectors are automatically authorized:

Distribution Sectors	Tourism Sectors
➤ Perfumery, beauty products and cosmetics	➤ Car rental
	➤ Areas of leisure
➤ Clothing	➤ Management of hotels
➤ Footwear	
➤ Leather goods	➤ **Training Sectors**
➤ Sports articles and shoes	➤ Professional training
➤ Diet products	
➤ Watches	➤ **Other economic sectors**
➤ Giftware items	➤ Rescue services
➤ Eyewear	➤ Beauty, hairdressing, and personal hygiene salons
➤ Household electrical appliances	➤ Repair and maintenance services (cars, electronics)
➤ Furniture	
➤ Indoor plants and flowers	➤ Services supporting efforts to quit smoking
➤ Sanitary items and hardware	➤ Care services in hotels
➤ Electronics and computer hardware	➤ Thalassotherapy

---

[3] This interpretation is confirmed by provisions of the Trade Minister Order which provide that, pursuant to Article 6 of the Competition Law, franchise agreements in the sectors noted in the table appended to the order, are granted an automatic authorization from the general prohibition of agreements and practices referred to in the Competition Law.

➢ Bookstores ➢ Capital goods for various sectors	

      e.   Potential Conflicts Under Tunisian Law

The automatic authorization of certain franchise agreements specified in the Decree and the Trade Minister Order, without verifying the fulfillment of the conditions of Article 6 of the Competition Law, squarely puts the Decree and the Trade Minister Order in conflict with the Competition Law. *Consequently, it is not prudent to assume that a franchise agreement will be granted automatic and general authorization without appealing to the Trade Minister for approval.*[4]

---

[4] A reading of the provisions of the 2009 Law, the Decree, the Trade Minister Order and the Competition Law suggest there is some potential conflict in Tunisian law that raises a number of important considerations.

The Decree suggests that certain franchise agreements in certain economic sectors, will be automatically authorized by the Trade Minister; however, Article 15 of the 2009 Law provides that the Decree shall only set forth the compulsory minimum terms of the franchise agreement and the required disclosures.

The 2009 Law regulates franchise agreements and places no restrictions on such agreements. In some cases, however, the Decree and Trade Minister Order limit the circumstances under which franchise agreements become effective. Consequently, the Decree and the Trade Minister Order may conflict with the 2009 Law and/or Article 6 of the Competition Law.

Further, the 2009 Law, the Decree and the Trade Minister Order do not address potential conflicts with the Competition Law. Specifically, the 2009 Law regulates franchise agreements without addressing potential conflicts with the general prohibitions against "anticompetitive practices, agreements and activities" of the Competition Law. Also, the "automatic authorization" granted by the Decree potentially conflicts with the general prohibitions against "anticompetitive practices, agreements and activities" of the Competition Law.

Tunisia

f.   Obtaining Trade Minister Authorization

In the event a franchisor is required to obtain authorization, there are specific documents that must be submitted to the Trade Minister including:

- an application in the form of a cover letter;

- a copy of the draft franchise agreement; and

- a technical and economic study showing that the franchise agreement is not anti-competitive, is necessary to guarantee technical or economic progress, and that it provides users with a fair share of benefits.

Again, it is important to note that this is an evolving area of Tunisian law and the interplay between the 2009 Law, the Decree, the Trade Minster Order and the Competition Law have yet to be determined. It is prudent to consult with local counsel in Tunisia to determine the applicability of the foregoing laws to specific circumstances and whether Trade Minister authorization will be required.

2.   The Central Bank of Tunisia's Prior Authorization

In principle, based on the Exchange Control Regulations in Tunisia (the "Regulations"), payments made by a resident to a party outside of Tunisia pursuant to an agreement are subject to the prior authorization of the Central Bank of Tunisia (the "CBT"). This means that, in principle, such agreement is itself subject to CBT's prior authorization.

The issue of whether payments made under a franchise agreement and whether such agreement is therefore subject to the authorization of the CBT is not clear under the Regulations.

Under the Regulations, there are two kinds of operations:

Tunisia

- "Current operations" where payments outside of Tunisia can be made freely without authorization (but following a specific procedure); and

- Other or "non-current operations" where payments outside of Tunisia require the prior authorization of the CBT.

Pursuant to the Regulations, current operations include payments made outside Tunisia in consideration of "…intellectual property rights like…the use of the trade name and the brand name." It is unclear whether the CBT will consider payments made under a franchise agreement as a current operation because payments under such an agreement must be related to "production" of goods as opposed to the use of a trademark.

Based on the foregoing, it is prudent for the parties to (i) seek confirmation that the payments to be made under their franchise agreement are current operations and (ii) seek authorization in case the CBT does not consider them as such.

There are no specific documents to be submitted to the CBT, but usually the application is made in the form of a cover letter with a draft of the franchise agreement appended. The CBT will examine the file and may request, if necessary, additional documents or information. In principle, the CBT gives its provisional approval on the draft franchise agreement, and once executed by the parties, the CBT gives its final authorization. Accordingly, the franchise agreement is, in principle, submitted again to the CBT once signed by the parties. The CBT will inform the parties about its final authorization.

The timeline for obtaining CBT authorization is approximately two months, but this timeline could be affected by several factors including the number of cases pending before the CBT. The CBT has the ability to reject the filing or modify its terms. Please note that there are no specific standards used to approve an agreement but the approval depends on the sector, the circumstances, the parties concerned, etc.

3. Registration before the Tax Office

A franchise agreement is not required to be registered with the Tax Office of Tunisia. However, registration, even though not mandatory, ensures enforceability against third parties.

C. Limits of Fees and Typical Term of Franchise Agreement

Please describe any limits upon the nature and extent of fees and the term of a typical franchise agreement.

There are no limits upon the nature and extent of fees and the term of a typical franchise agreement.

III. Currency

If all payments under a franchise agreement must be made in immediately available U.S. Dollars, please advise as to any restrictions, reporting requirements, or regulations concerning the exchange, repatriation, or remittance of U.S. Dollars.

Based on the Regulations, any payments, regardless of the currency, made by a resident franchisee to a party outside of Tunisia, pursuant to a franchise agreement, are likely subject to the authorization of the Central Bank of Tunisia. See Section II.B.2.

IV. Taxes, Tariffs and Duties

Please do not provide any in-depth comments on tax structuring. However, please provide your general comments on the typical amount of withholding tax that would apply and whether a "gross-up" provision contained in a franchise agreement would be enforceable in your country.

If the franchise agreement is registered with the Tax Office, as mentioned in Section II.B.1. above, a duty of 20 Tunisian dinars

Tunisia

(approximately US$ 12.50) per page (including the pages of all the originals presented for registration) will be due.

Moreover, payments due under the franchise agreement are subject to:

- a value added tax ("VAT") of 18%; and

- A 15% withholding tax calculated on the amounts paid, including the VAT, whether the franchisor is established in or outside of Tunisia.

Tunisia has double taxation treaties with a number of jurisdictions, including the United States.[5]

Any "gross up" provisions contained in franchise agreements are enforceable in Tunisia.

V.   Trademarks

Please advise us as to whether there are any special requirements for granting a valid trademark license, including the use of a registered user agreement or a short trademark license agreement and any required filing of such an agreement with the trademark authorities.

There are special requirements under Tunisian law for granting a trademark license. Such a license could be deemed to fall under the purview of Article 14 of the 2009 Law because this legislation defines the franchise agreement as a contract through

---

[5] Tunisia has double taxation treaties with Algeria, Arab Maghreb Union, Austria, Belgium, Burkina Faso, Canada, China, Czech Republic, Denmark, Egypt, Ethiopia, France, Germany, Great Britain, Greece, Hungary, Indonesia, Iraq, Iran, Italy, Jordan, Korea, Kuwait, Lebanon, Libya, Luxembourg, Mali, Malta, Mauritania, Morocco, Netherlands, Norway, Pakistan, Poland, Portugal, Oman, Qatar, Romania, Senegal, South Africa, Spain, Sudan, Sweden, Switzerland, Syria, Turkey, U.A.E., United States and Yemen.

Tunisia

which the trademark owner[6] grants the right to use the mark to a natural person or to a legal entity.

In Tunisia, trademark ownership is established through registration of the trademark with the National Institute for Standardization and Industrial Property (*Institut National de la Normalisation et de la Propriété Industrielle*). The trademark's registration number must be referenced in the franchise agreement and registered with the National Institute of Standardization and Industrial Property in order for franchisee's and franchisor's rights to be enforceable against third parties.

VI.   Restrictions on Transfer

Please advise as to whether there are any restrictions (1) on a franchisor to restrict transfers by a master franchisee, any transfer of interest in a master franchisee, or the assets of the master franchisee or (2) the ability of a master franchisee to control and/or restrict transfers of a subfranchisee's rights under a master franchise agreement, interest in the subfranchisee, or the assets of the subfranchisee.

There are no restrictions:

- on a franchisor's ability to restrict transfers by a master franchisee, any transfer of interest in a master franchisee, or transfer of any assets of the master franchisee; or

- on the ability of a master franchisee to control and/or restrict transfers of a subfranchisee's rights under a master franchise agreement, any interest in the subfranchisee, or any assets of the subfranchisee.

---

[6]   Article 16 of the 2009 Law provides that the franchisor must be the owner of the trademark.

VII. Termination

Please advise us as to any laws relating to termination in your country, such as agency laws, required indemnity provisions, notice or "good cause" requirements, or other laws affecting termination of a franchise agreement. Please describe.

A. Termination from the Competition Law Perspective

In some instances, the Tunisian Competition Council may consider the termination of a commercial relationship by the franchisor as anticompetitive. It may prevent the franchisor from terminating a franchise agreement, without an objective reason.

The illegal abuse of a party's state of economic dependency is one reason that may be cited as a cause of termination and such terminations are prohibited under the Competition Law. According to such law, it is considered an abuse of third parties' state of economic dependency to terminate an agreement without cause or to terminate because the other party refused to accept exorbitant commercial conditions. If such a violation of the law is found, the Competition Law (and thus the Tunisian Competition Council) may invalidate the franchise agreement irrespective of the choice of the law and the choice of dispute resolution agreed to between the parties. Moreover, the Competition Law may subject the franchisor to sanctions (e.g., fines).

From a Competition Law perspective, a state of economic dependency exists only if the franchisee is unable to conduct any business without the involvement of the franchisor due to some or all of the following:

- the brand notoriety of the franchisor;

- the market share of the franchisor;

Tunisia

- the franchisor's share of the turnover of the franchisee; or

- the absence of equivalent solutions (e.g. business alternatives) for the franchisee.

Where the franchisee has an exclusive arrangement with the franchisor, the state of economic dependency is more easily proved. However, even the question of the legality of exclusivity is not clear-cut under Tunisian law. Some jurists consider that all forms of exclusivity are forbidden in Tunisia, despite the fact that certain sectors continue to operate under exclusive arrangements.

B.   Termination under the Insolvency Legal Regime

Under Tunisian law, if a franchisee is experiencing financial difficulties, it is sometimes determined that certain outstanding contracts (such as a franchise agreement) concluded with such an entity cannot be terminated. This is a matter of public policy and overrules all the provisions of the law applicable to the franchise agreement, and the dispute resolution agreed to between the parties.

C.   Termination from a Civil Law Perspective

The Competition Law deals only with offenses against competition, and sanctions such offenses by various penalties (e.g., fines). If the Tunisian Competition Council determines that the franchisor abused the state of economic dependency of the franchisee, the franchisee may bring a civil lawsuit before the Tunisian civil courts to claim compensation for damages suffered. Such a lawsuit is based on the tort caused to the franchisee and may be brought before the Tunisian courts, notwithstanding the choice of the law and the choice of dispute resolution agreed between the parties.[7]

The courts may award compensation in favor of the franchisee. Such an award is intended to allow the franchisee to reorganize itself and to find other commercial opportunities.

VIII. Governing Law, Jurisdiction, and Dispute Resolution

A.   Choice of Law of Foreign Jurisdiction

Please confirm whether the choice of law of a foreign jurisdiction would likely to be upheld under the law of the country, except for certain matters such as trademarks, bankruptcy, and competition matters, which we assume would be governed by the law in your country.

Except the matters mentioned in Section VII above and certain other matters, such as exchange control issues, that would be governed by Tunisian law, the choice of law of a foreign jurisdiction in a franchise agreement would be upheld under the laws of Tunisia. Article 62 of the Tunisian Code of International Private law provides that the contract (e.g. a franchise agreement) is governed by the law chosen by the parties. If the parties have not chosen a governing law, and if the contract concerns a professional or commercial activity, the law to be taken into consideration is the law of the country where the party whose contractual obligation is being determined is domiciled or where that party has a principal office. Moreover, Article 69 of the Code provides that contracts related to intellectual property are governed by the law of the country of the person who

---

[7] The *Tunisian Code of International Private Law* was adopted by Law *n° 98-97* dated November 27, 1998. Article 5, paragraph 1 of the Code provides that: "Tunisian courts are also competent to judge…the cases based on tort if the act which caused the damage or the damage itself occurred in Tunisia."

transferred or relinquished the intellectual property rights unless a different governing law is chosen by the parties.

B.   International Arbitration Dispute Resolution

Please confirm that a court in your country would honor an election of international arbitration dispute resolution, and therefore refuse to hear any disputes arising under a franchise agreement.

Except the matters mentioned in Section VII above and certain other matters, such as exchange control issues, that would be governed by Tunisian courts, a court in Tunisia would honor an election of an international arbitration dispute resolution and refuse to hear any dispute arising under a franchise agreement.

Based on Article 52 of the *Tunisian Arbitration Code*,[8] a Tunisian court that considers a matter subject to an arbitration agreement must refer the parties to arbitration, if one of the parties so requests. The request must be made no later than the day the party presents to the court its statement on the substance of the matter, unless it appears to the court that the arbitration agreement is void, ineffective or cannot be enforced. Article 53 of the same code provides that when such a lawsuit is brought before a court, and the matter was not yet referred to the arbitration court, the court must declare itself incompetent, unless it appears that the arbitration agreement is clearly void.

An arbitration agreement may be considered clearly void when for example it was the result of outright fraud (i.e., forgery of a signature); if one of the parties to the agreement did not have the capacity or the power to sign the agreement or when the arbitration agreement was signed under duress.

---

[8]   The *Tunisian Arbitration Code* was adopted by the *law n° 93-42* dated April 26, 1993.

Tunisia

The court cannot declare its incompetence automatically if none of the parties put forward the arbitration agreement.

It is important to note that Article 54 of the *Tunisian Arbitration Code* provides that a party may request a temporary protective measure (i.e., the seizure of assets or inventory) from a court before the matter is referred to the arbitration.

Tunisia gives effect to some provisions of the *Convention on the Recognition and Enforcement of Foreign Arbitral Awards* (the "New York Convention") – to which it is a signatory.

IX.   Non-Competition Provisions

If the franchise agreement prohibits the franchisee from engaging in certain competitive activities during the term of the agreement, and for a 12-month period after the termination or expiration of the agreement, please comment on the enforceability of non-competition covenants in your country.

Because non-competition clauses are recognized and enforceable under Tunisian law, the franchise agreement may prohibit the franchisee from engaging in certain competitive activities during the term of the contract, and for a 12-month period after the termination or expiration of the contract. Article 118 of the Tunisian Civil Code (*Code des Obligations et des Contrats*) permits restraints on exercising a certain commerce or industry, in a specified location or for a specific duration.

X.   Language Requirements

Does the law in your country require that a franchise agreement be translated into the local language in order to be enforceable between the parties?

Tunisian law does not require that a franchise agreement be translated into the local language to be enforceable between the parties. However, it must be translated into the local language,

Tunisia

(in principle by a sworn translator in Tunisia), if the franchise agreement is:

- registered before the Tax Office (as mentioned in Section II.B.1. above);

- filed with any administration (as mentioned in Section III above); or

- presented to Tunisian courts for any reason.

XI. Other Significant Matters

Please advise as to whether there are any significant matters not addressed above of which a franchisor should be aware in connection with its entering into a franchise agreement in your country.

Article 15 of the 2009 Law provides that the compulsory minimum terms of the franchise agreement are set by decree. Article 2 of the Decree provides that the franchise agreements must include the rights and obligations of the franchisor and the franchisee, and notably the following information:

- services provided by the franchisor to the franchisee and notably the transfer of know-how, technical expertise, and use of intellectual property rights;

- remunerations required from the franchisee;

- term of the franchise agreement and the conditions of its renewal;

- conditions of use of the trademark or the corporate name;

- conditions of the termination of the franchise agreement;

- conditions of the exclusivity of supply;

- non-competition conditions;

- delineation of the geographical area of the exclusive use of the trademark or the corporate name;

- franchisee's obligation to keep confidential the information disclosed by the franchisor;

- investment plan to be realized by the franchisee;

- mechanisms on the basis of which the advertising expenses are shared;

- communication to the franchisor regarding the sales and the financial situation of the franchisee;

- conditions under which the franchisor or its representatives have access to franchisee's premises;

- possibility of the franchisee to subfranchise with third parties in respect of each geographical area, in case the franchise agreement is exclusive for the entire territory of Tunisia.

Article 4 of the Decree provides also that the franchise agreement shall not contain anticompetitive clauses intended to:

- impose sale or service prices on franchisee;

- fix a minimum turnover to be realized by the franchisee.

Article 16 of the 2009 Law requires that, during the franchise agreement term, the franchisor must provide to the franchisee the necessary commercial and technical assistance and all material information related to the franchise network.

Article 16 of the 2009 Law also requires that the franchisee must provide to the franchisor information relating to the sales realized and its financial situation. It authorizes the franchisor or its representatives to inspect the franchisee's business premises during the typical work or operating hours.

Tunisia

Bibliography of International Franchise Resources

Kendal H. Tyre, Jr., Diana Vilmenay-Hammond, Pierce Haesung Han, Courtney L. Lindsay, II and Keri McWilliams

Nixon Peabody LLP

Washington, D.C.

I.　General International Resources

Mark Abell, Gary R. Duvall, and Andrea Oricchio Kirsh, *International Franchise Legislation* B1, ABA FORUM ON FRANCHISING (1996)

Kathleen C. Anderson and Anthony M. Stiegler, *Put Muscle in Your Marks: Enforcing Intellectual Property Rights* W14, ABA FORUM ON FRANCHISING (1995)

Richard M. Asbill and Jane W. LaFranchi, *International Franchise Sales Laws—A Survey* W7, ABA FORUM ON FRANCHISING (2005)

Jeffery A. Brimer, Alison C. McElroy, and John Pratt, *Going International: What Additional Restraints Will You Face?* W4, ABA FORUM ON FRANCHISING (2011)

Michael G. Brennan, Alexander Konigsberg, and Philip F. Zeidman, *Globetrotting: A Workshop on International Franchising* 10/W8, ABA FORUM ON FRANCHISING (1994)

Michael G. Brennan, Alexander Konigsberg, and Philip F. Zeidman, *Globetrotting: Strategies for Launching U.S. Franchisors Abroad* 2/P2, ABA FORUM ON FRANCHISING (1994)

Christopher P. Bussert and Jennifer Dolman, *Regaining Your Trademark After Abandonment or Misappropriation* W7, ABA FORUM ON FRANCHISING (2011)

Ronald T. Coleman and Linda K. Stevens, *Trade Secrets and Confidential Information: Rights and Remedies* W2, ABA FORUM ON FRANCHISING (2000)

Finola Cunningham, *Commerce Department Helps Franchisors Go Global*, in FRANCHISING WORLD 63 (Dec. 2005)

Michael R. Daigle and Alex S. Konigsberg, *Meeting Off-Shore Disclosure and Contract Requirements* F/W13, ABA FORUM ON FRANCHISING (1992)

Jennifer Dolman, Robert A. Lauer, and Lawrence M. Weinberg, *Structuring International Master Franchise Relationships for Success and Responding When Things Go Awry* W22, ABA FORUM ON FRANCHISING (2007)

Gary R. Duvall, Paul Jones, and Jane LaFranchi, *Planning for the International Enforcement of Franchise Agreements* W6, ABA FORUM ON FRANCHISING (1999)

William Edwards, *International Expansion: Do Opportunities Outweigh Challenges?* in FRANCHISING WORLD (February 2008)

George J. Eydt and Stuart Hershman, *Bringing a Foreign Franchise System to the United States* W9, ABA FORUM ON FRANCHISING (2009)

William A. Finkelstein and Louis T. Pirkey, *International Trademarks* W15, ABA FORUM ON FRANCHISING (1991)

William A. Finkelstein, *Protecting Trademarks Internationally: Current Strategies and Developments* B3, ABA FORUM ON FRANCHISING (1996)

Stephen Giles, Lou H. Jones, and Lawrence Weinberg, *Negotiating and Documenting Complex International Franchise Agreements* W21, ABA FORUM ON FRANCHISING (2006)

Steven M. Goldman, Stephen Giles, Marc Israel, and Stanley Wong, *Competition Round Up from Around the World* LB2, ABA FORUM ON FRANCHISING (2004)

David C. Gryce and E. Lynn Perry, *Trademarks and Copyrights in the International Arena* 6/W4, ABA FORUM ON FRANCHISING (1993)

Kenneth S. Kaplan, Andrew P. Loewinger, and Penelope J. Ward, *System Standards in International Franchising* W14, ABA FORUM ON FRANCHISING (2005)

Edward Levitt and Jorge Mondragon, *A Survey of International Legal Traps and How to Avoid Them—Beyond the Franchise Laws* W20, ABA FORUM ON FRANCHISING (2007)

Ned Levitt, Kendal H. Tyre, and Penny Ward, *The Impossible Dream: Controlling Your International Franchise System* W4, ABA FORUM ON FRANCHISING (2010)

Michael K. Lindsey and Andrew P. Loewinger, *International (Non-U.S.) Franchise Disclosure Requirements* W9, ABA FORUM ON FRANCHISING (2002)

Andrew P. Loewinger and John Pratt, *Recent Changes and Trends in International Franchise Laws* W4, ABA FORUM ON FRANCHISING (2008)

Andrew P. Loewinger and Thomas M. Pitegoff, *Avoiding the Long Arm of the Law in International Franchising: Issues and Approaches* W8, ABA FORUM ON FRANCHISING (1995)

Craig J. Madson and Katherine C. Spelman, *Similarity and Confusion in the Intellectual Property Arena* W11, ABA FORUM ON FRANCHISING (1997)

Christopher A. Nowak, John Pratt, and Carl E. Zwisler, *Franchising Internationally with Countries with Opaque Legal Systems* W20, ABA FORUM ON FRANCHISING (2006)

E. Lynn Perry and John L. Sullivan Jr., *Trademark Compliance and Enforcement Techniques* E/W12, ABA FORUM ON FRANCHISING (1992)

Marcel Portmann, *Franchising Sector Proves Global Reach*, in FRANCHISING WORLD (January 2007)

John Pratt and Luiz Henrique O. do Amaral, *Civil Law for Common Law Practitioners (or How to Draft an Agreement for Use Overseas)* W4, ABA FORUM ON FRANCHISING (2002)

Kirk W. Reilly, Robert F. Salkowski and Geoffrey B. Shaw, *Determining the Rules of Engagement in Litigation Here and Abroad* W5, ABA FORUM ON FRANCHISING (2008)

Catherine Riesterer and Frank Zaid, *Basics of International Franchising* L/B2, ABA FORUM ON FRANCHISING (1997)

W. Andrew Scott and Christopher N. Wormald, *Stranger in a Strange Land: Contrasting Franchising in International Expansion* W2, ABA FORUM ON FRANCHISING (2003)

Donald Smith and Erik Wulff, *International Franchising: The Unraveling of an International Franchise Relationship* 15/W13, ABA FORUM ON FRANCHISING (1993)

Frank Zaid, Pamela Mills, and Michael Santa Maria, *Essential Issues in International Franchising* LB/1, ABA FORUM ON FRANCHISING (2001)

II. African Resources

Joyce G. Mazero and J. Perry Maisonneuve, *Franchising in the Middle East and North Africa* W2, ABA FORUM ON FRANCHISING (2009)

Kendal H. Tyre, Jr. and Diana Vilmenay-Hammond, *Franchise World: A Burgeoning Middle Class Spurs Franchise Investment in Africa*, MINORITY BUSINESS ENTREPRENEUR (November 2012)

Kendal H. Tyre, Jr., *IP Protection May Promote Additional Franchise Growth in Africa*, NIXON PEABODY LLP: FRANCHISING BUSINESS & LAW ALERT (September 2012)

Kendal H. Tyre, Jr., *Market Potential for Franchising in Africa*, NIXON PEABODY LLP: FRANCHISING BUSINESS & LAW ALERT (June 2011)

Kendal H. Tyre, Jr. and Courtney L. Lindsay, II, *Continued Growth of Franchising in Africa*, NIXON PEABODY LLP: FRANCHISE LAW ALERT (April 2013)

Kendal H. Tyre, Jr. and Courtney L. Lindsay, II, *Pan African Franchise Federation Holds Inaugural Meeting*, NIXON PEABODY LLP: AFRICA ALERT (June 2013)

Kendal H. Tyre, Jr. and Courtney L. Lindsay, II, *White House Encouraging Private Investment and Transparency in Sub-Saharan Africa*, NIXON PEABODY LLP: AFRICA ALERT (August 2012)

Kendal H. Tyre, Jr. and Diana Vilmenay-Hammond, *African Economic Growth Impacts Franchising on the Continent*, NIXON PEABODY LLP: FRANCHISE LAW ALERT (July 2012)

Kendal H. Tyre, Jr. and Diana Vilmenay-Hammond, *Franchising in Africa*, in FRANCHISING WORLD (August 2013)

John Sotos and Sam Hall, *African Franchising: Cross-Continent Momentum*, in FRANCHISING WORLD (June 2007)

A. Angola

João Afonso Fialho, *Franchising in Angola*, in FRANCHISING IN AFRICA: LEGAL AND BUSINESS CONSIDERATIONS 91-105 (Kendal H. Tyre, Jr. & Diana Vilmenay-Hammond eds. 2012)

27

B. Botswana

Bonzo Makgalemele, *Franchising in Botswana*, in FRANCHISING IN AFRICA: LEGAL AND BUSINESS CONSIDERATIONS 107-117 (Kendal H. Tyre, Jr. & Diana Vilmenay-Hammond eds. 2012)

C. Cape Verde

João Afonso Fialho, *Franchising in Cape Verde*, in FRANCHISING IN AFRICA: LEGAL AND BUSINESS CONSIDERATIONS 119-132 (Kendal H. Tyre, Jr. & Diana Vilmenay-Hammond eds. 2012)

D. Egypt

Girgis Abd El-Shahid, *Franchising in Eqypt*, in FRANCHISING IN AFRICA: LEGAL AND BUSINESS CONSIDERATIONS 133-142 (Kendal H. Tyre, Jr. & Diana Vilmenay-Hammond eds. 2012)

A. Safaa El Din El Oteifi, *Egypt*, in INTERNATIONAL FRANCHISING EGY/1 (Dennis Campbell gen. ed. 2011)

E. Ethiopia

Yohannes Assefa and Biset Beyene Molla, *Franchising in Ethiopia*, in FRANCHISING IN AFRICA: LEGAL AND BUSINESS CONSIDERATIONS 143-157 (Kendal H. Tyre, Jr. & Diana Vilmenay-Hammond eds. 2012)

Kendal H. Tyre, Jr., Yohannes Assefa and Getachew Mengistie Alemu, *New Intellectual Property Regulation Requires Scramble to Protect Marks in Ethiopia*, NIXON PEABODY LLP: AFRICA ALERT (October 2013)

F. Ghana

Divine K.D. Letsa and Hawa Tejansie Ajei, *Franchising in Ghana*, in FRANCHISING IN AFRICA: LEGAL AND BUSINESS CONSIDERATIONS 159-167 (Kendal H. Tyre, Jr. & Diana Vilmenay-Hammond eds. 2012)

G. Libya

Kendal H. Tyre, Jr. & Diana Vilmenay-Hammond, *First U.S. Franchise Opens in Libya*, NIXON PEABODY LLP: AFRICA ALERT (August 2012)

H. Mozambique

Diogo Xavier da Cunha, *Franchising in Mozambique*, in FRANCHISING IN AFRICA: LEGAL AND BUSINESS CONSIDERATIONS 169-182 (Kendal H. Tyre, Jr. & Diana Vilmenay-Hammond eds. 2012)

I. Nigeria

Theo Emuwa and Bimbola Fowler-Ekar, *Franchising in Nigeria*, in FRANCHISING IN AFRICA: LEGAL AND BUSINESS CONSIDERATIONS 183-198 (Kendal H. Tyre, Jr. & Diana Vilmenay-Hammond eds. 2012)

Kendal H. Tyre, Jr. and Theo Emuwa, *Nigerian Franchising: Making Your Way Through the Thicket*, NIXON PEABODY LLP: FRANCHISE LAW ALERT (June 2005)

J. South Africa

Eugene Honey, *Franchising and the New Consumer Protection Bill*, BOWMAN GILFILLAN (March 2008)

Eugene Honey, *Franchising and the Consumer Protection Bill*, BOWMAN GILFILLAN (May 2008)

Eugene Honey, *Pitfalls and Difficulties with the CPA*, ADAMS & ADAMS (March 2013)

Eugene Honey, *Disclosure is Compulsory*, ADAMS & ADAMS (May 2013)

Eugene Honey and Wim Alberts, *Fundamental Consumer Rights: The Right to Equality*, BOWMAN GILFILLAN (March 2009)

Eugene Honey and Wim Alberts, *The Reach of the Consumer Protection Bill: The Final*, BOWMAN GILFILLAN (March 2009)

Eugene Honey, *South Africa*, in GETTING THE DEAL THROUGH: FRANCHISE (2013) 172-178 (Philip F. Zeidman ed. 2013)

Taswell Papier, *Franchising in South Africa*, in FRANCHISING IN AFRICA: LEGAL AND BUSINESS CONSIDERATIONS 199-224 (Kendal H. Tyre, Jr. & Diana Vilmenay-Hammond eds. 2012)

Kendal H. Tyre, Jr., *A New Legal Landscape for Franchising in South Africa*, NIXON PEABODY LLP: FRANCHISING BUSINESS & LAW ALERT (September 2009)

K.   Tunisia

Yessine Ferah, *Franchising in Tunisia*, in FRANCHISING IN AFRICA: LEGAL AND BUSINESS CONSIDERATIONS 225-245 (Kendal H. Tyre, Jr. & Diana Vilmenay-Hammond eds. 2012)

Kendal H. Tyre, Jr., Diana Vilmenay-Hammond, and Yessine Ferah, *New Franchise Legislation in Tunisia*, NIXON PEABODY LLP: FRANCHISE LAW ALERT (September 2010)

L.   Zambia

Mabvuto Sakala, *Franchising in Zambia*, in FRANCHISING IN AFRICA: LEGAL AND BUSINESS CONSIDERATIONS 247-255 (Kendal H. Tyre, Jr. & Diana Vilmenay-Hammond eds. 2012)

14764570.1

www.ingramcontent.com/pod-product-compliance
Lightning Source LLC
Chambersburg PA
CBHW060324220326
41598CB00027B/4419